REFLECTIONS
of
ROMANTIC LOVE

REFLECTIONS

of

Romantic Love

COMPILED BY JOHN HADFIELD

PICTURES FROM THE TATE GALLERY

A GRAHAM TARRANT BOOK

DAVID & CHARLES
Newton Abbot · London · North Pomfret (Vt)

Designed by Julia Alldridge Associates
Cover paper design by courtesy of the Italian Paper Shop, London

British Library Cataloguing in Publication Data

Reflections of romantic love.—(A Graham Tarrant book)
1. English literature   2. Love—Literary
collections
I. Hadfield, John, *1907–*   II. Tate Gallery
820.8′0354   PR1111.L7

ISBN 0-7153-8847-9

Typeset by Typesetters (Birmingham) Ltd,
Smethwick, West Midlands
and printed in The Netherlands
by Royal Smeets Offset, Weert
for David & Charles Publishers plc
Brunel House   Newton Abbot   Devon

Published in the United States of America
by David & Charles Inc
North Pomfret   Vermont 05053   USA

IT WAS evening when I met her, and the sun was setting up the Brecon road. I was walking by the almshouses when there came down the steps a tall slight beautiful girl with a graceful figure and long flowing fair hair. Her lovely face was delicately pale, her features refined and aristocratic and her eyes a soft dark tender blue. She looked at me earnestly, longingly and lovingly, and dropped a pretty courtesy. Florence, Florence Hill, sweet Florence Hill, is it you? Once more. Thank God. Once more. My darling, my darling. As she stood and lifted those blue eyes, those soft dark loving eyes shyly to mine, it seemed to me as if the doors and windows of heaven were suddenly opened. It was one of the supreme moments of life. As I stood by the roadside holding her hand, lost to all else and conscious only of her presence, I was in heaven already, or if still on earth in the body, the flights of golden stairs sloped to my feet and one of the angels had come down to me. Florence, Florence Hill, my darling, my darling. It was well nigh all I could say in my emotion. With one long lingering loving look and clasp of the hand we parted and I saw her no more.

THE REVEREND FRANCIS KILVERT
Diary, 23 March 1874

ARTHUR HUGHES
Aurora Leigh's Dismissal of Romney ('The Tryst'), 1860

Ah! may'st thou ever be what now thou art,
Nor unbeseem the promise of thy spring,
As fair in form, as warm yet pure in heart,
Love's image upon earth without his wing,
And guileless beyond Hope's imagining!
And surely she who now so fondly rears
Thy youth, in thee, thus hourly brightening,
Beholds the rainbow of her future years,
Before whose heavenly hues all sorrow disappears . . .

GEORGE GORDON, BARON BYRON
'To Ianthe, A Dedication', *Childe Harold's Pilgrimage*, 1812

JAMES ABBOT MCNEILL WHISTLER
Miss Cicely Alexander: Harmony in Grey and Green, 1872

I ne'er was struck before that hour
  With love so sudden and so sweet.
Her face it bloomed like a sweet flower
  And stole my heart away complete.
My face turned pale as deadly pale,
  My legs refused to walk away,
And when she looked 'what could I ail?'
  My life and all seemed turned to clay.

And then my blood rushed to my face
  And took my sight away.
The trees and bushes round the place
  Seemed midnight at noonday.
I could not see a single thing,
  Words from my eyes did start;
They spoke as chords do from the string,
  And blood burnt round my heart.

Are flowers the winter's choice?
  Is Love's bed always snow?
She seemed to hear my silent voice
  And love's appeal to know.
I never saw so sweet a face
  As that I stood before:
My heart has left its dwelling-place
  And can return no more.

JOHN CLARE
Poems, 1920 (written 1842–64)

GEORGE ROMNEY
A Lady in a Brown Dress, c 1785

A ND WHILE they were talking, Hilda, in her head, was writing a fervent letter to him: ". . . You see it was so sudden. I had had no chance to tell you. I did so want to tell you, but how could I? And I hadn't told anybody! I'm sure you will agree with me that it is best to tell some things as little as possible. And when you had kissed me, how could I tell you then – at once? I could not. It would have spoiled everything. Surely you understand. I know you do, because you understand everything. If I was wrong, tell me where. You don't guess how humble I am! When I think of you, I am the humblest girl you can imagine . . ."

ARNOLD BENNETT
Hilda Lessways, 1911

WILLIAM STRANG
Bank Holiday, 1912

When she rises in the morning
I linger to watch her;
She spreads the bath-cloth underneath the window
And the sunbeams catch her
Glistening white on the shoulders,
While down her sides the mellow
Golden shadow glows as
She stoops to the sponge, and her swung breasts
Sway like full-blown yellow
Gloire de Dijon roses.

She drips herself with water, and her shoulders
Glisten as silver, they crumple up
Like wet and falling roses, and I listen
For the sluicing of their rain-dishevelled petals.
In the window full of sunlight
Concentrates her golden shadow
Fold on fold, until it glows as
Mellow as the glory roses.

D H LAWRENCE
'Gloire de Dijon', *Look, We Have Come Through!* 1917

EDGAR DEGAS
Woman in a Tub, c 1885

Bright through the valley gallops the brooklet;
　　Over the welkin travels the cloud;
Touched by the zephyr, dances the harebell;
　　Cuckoo sits somewhere, singing so loud;
Swift o'er the meadows glitter the starlings,
　　Striking their wings, all the flock at a stroke;
Under the chestnuts new bees are swarming,
　　Rising and falling like magical smoke.
Two little children, seeing and hearing,
　　Hand in hand wander, shout, laugh, and sing;
Lo, in their bosoms, wild with the marvel,
　　Love, like the crocus, is come ere the Spring.
Young men and women, noble and tender,
　　Yearn for each other, faith truly plight,
Promise to cherish, comfort and honour;
　　Vow that makes duty one with delight.
Oh, but the glory, found in no story,
　　Radiance of Eden unquenched by the Fall;
Few may remember, none may reveal it,
　　This the first first-love, the first love of all!

COVENTRY PATMORE
Tamerton Church-Tower, and other Poems, 1853

JAMES CLARKE HOOK
Young Dreams, 1887 (detail)

Whilst thousands court fair Chloe's love,
    She fears the dangerous joy,
But, Cynthia-like, frequents the grove,
    As lovely, and as coy.

With the same speed she seeks the hind,
    Or hunts the flying hare,
She leaves pursuing swains behind,
    To languish and despair.

Oh strange caprice in thy dear breast!
    Whence first this whim began;
To follow thus each worthless beast,
    And shun their sovereign, man!

Consider, Fair, what 'tis you do,
    How thus they both must die,
Not surer they, when you pursue,
    Than we, whene'er you fly.

SOAME JENYNS
'Chloe Hunting', *Poems*, 1752

JOHN WOOTTON
Lady Mary Churchill at the Death of the Hare, 1748 (detail)

You that think Love can convey
    No other way
But through the eyes, into the heart,
    His fatal dart,
Close up those casements, and but hear
    This syren sing;
    And on the wing
Of her sweet voice it shall appear
That Love can enter at the ear.

Then unveil your eyes; behold
    The curious mould
Where that voice dwells, and as we know,
    When the cocks crow,
And Sol is mounted on his way,
    We freely may
    Gaze on the day;
So may you, when the music's done,
Awake, and see the rising sun.

THOMAS CAREW
'Celia Singing', *Poems*, 1640

SIR PETER LELY
A Lady of the Lake Family, c 1660 (detail)

Behold, thou art fair, my love; behold, thou art fair . . .
As the lily among thorns, so is my love among the daughters . . .
Thou has dove's eyes within thy locks . . .
Thy lips are like a thread of scarlet, and thy speech is comely . . .
Thy temples are like a piece of a pomegranate within thy locks . . .
Thou art all fair, my love . . . there is no spot in thee . . .
Thou hast ravished my heart with one of thine eyes,
    With one chain of thy neck . . .
How much better is thy love than wine, and the smell
    of thine ointments than all spices . . .
Thy lips, O my spouse, drop as the honeycomb: honey and
    milk are under thy tongue.

Lines from THE SONG OF SOLOMON

DANTE GABRIEL ROSSETTI
The Beloved, 1865–6

Do not ask me, charming Phillis,
　　Why I lead you here alone,
By this bank of pinks and lilies
　　And of roses newly blown.

'Tis not to behold the beauty
　　Of those flowers that crown the Spring;
'Tis to – but I know my duty,
　　And dare never name the thing.

('Tis, at worst, but her denying;
　　Why should I thus fearful be?
Every minute, gently flying,
　　Smiles and says, 'Make use of me.')

What the sun does to those roses,
　　While the beams play sweetly in,
I would – but my fear opposes,
　　And I dare not name the thing.

Yet I die, if I conceal it;
　　Ask my eyes, or ask your own;
And if neither can reveal it,
　　Think what lovers think alone.

On this bank of pinks and lilies,
　　Might I speak what I would do;
I would with my lovely Phillis –
　　I would; I would – Ah! would *you*?

ANONYMOUS
in *The Hive*, 1724

FRANCIS COTES
Portrait of a Lady, 1768

How happy could I be with either,
   Were t'other dear charmer away!
But while you thus teaze me together,
   To neither a word will I say.

But tol-de-rol, lol-de-rol-laddie
Te-rol-de-rol, lol-de-rol-ay!
But tol-de-rol, lol-de-rol-laddie
Te-rol-de-rol, lol-de-roy-ay!

JOHN GAY
The Beggar's Opera, 1728

JAMES TISSOT
Portsmouth Dockyard, c 1877 (detail)

DURING the fleeting weeks of that single summer, I lived through my first experience of intense love. All the poetry in my nature centred itself with sudden passion upon a single girl. For me she was the sun and moon, the sea, the hills, and the rivers, the cornfields, the hayfields, the plough-lands, and the first stars of nightfall. Everything that is lovely in nature became illumined by the thought of her: the garden at dawn, as I saw it looking down from the nursery window on the Round-beds and the Crescent-bed, populated with cold, diffident flowers: the meadows by the stream, so hushed in the night air, heavy with the scents of honeysuckle hedges and disturbed only by an occasional deep sighing from one of the ruminating cattle, with weighty body of warm flesh recumbent upon wet summer grass.

From the moment I had seen her in the church I could think of nothing else. My whole approach to life was altered. I no longer cared whether I was to be a poet or not a poet, I no longer was concerned with the deeper problems of existence. Unless I could associate what I saw, heard, tasted, smelt, and touched with her I no longer gave it attention. What reason was there for me to heed the waves that broke day and night against the irregular coasts of the world, to exult in the grass that grew day and night upon the broad back of the stationary land, to watch from ancient elbow-bone bridges the flowing away of rivers, to look up at the crafty midnight stars, unless such appearances could be made to serve in some way as poetical settings for this girl of my utter idolatry? It seemed to me then, as indeed it seems to me still, that every inch of her body shone with some mysterious light . . . that she breathed, that she walked, that she slept to wake again, was an unending source of wonder to me.

LLEWELYN POWYS
Love and Death, 1939

ARTHUR HUGHES
April Love, 1955–6

In vain, dear Chloe, you suggest
That I, inconstant, have possessed
   Or loved a fairer she:
Would you with ease at once be cured
Of all the ills you've long endured,
   Consult your glass and me.

If then you think that I can find
A nymph more fair, or one more kind,
   You've reason for your fears:
But if impartial you will prove
To your own beauty and my love,
   How needless are your tears! . . .

With wanton flight the curious bee
From flower to flower still wanders free,
   And, where each blossom blows,
Extracts the juice of all he meets,
But for his quintessence of sweets
   He ravishes the rose.

So my fond fancy to employ
On each variety of joy
   From nymph to nymph I roam;
Perhaps see fifty in a day;
Those are but visits which I pay –
   For Chloe is my home!

SIR WILLIAM YONGE
in James Ralph's *Miscellaneous Poems*, 1729

PETER ANGELLIS (1685–1735)
Conversation Piece (detail)

My lady seems of ivory
Forehead, straight nose, and cheeks that be
Hollow'd a little mournfully.
                    Beata mea Domina!

Her forehead, overshadow'd much
By bows of hair, has a wave such
As God was good to make for me.
                    Beata mea Domina! . . .

Beneath her brows the lids fall slow,
The lashes a clear shadow throw
Where I would wish my lips to be.
                    Beata mea Domina!

Her great eyes, standing far apart,
Draw up some memory from her heart,
And gaze out very mournfully;
                    Beata mea Domina!

So beautiful and kind they are,
But most times looking out afar,
Waiting for something, not for me.
                    Beata mea Domina! . . .

Lurking below the underlid,
Darkening the place where they lie hid –
If they should rise and flow for me!
                    Beata mea Domina! . . .

WILLIAM MORRIS
'Praise of My Lady', 1858

WILLIAM MORRIS
Queen Guinevere, 1858
(The model was Jane Burden, who became Morris's wife)

AMID the gloom and travail of existence suddenly to behold a beautiful being, and as instantaneously to feel an overwhelming conviction that with that fair form for ever our destiny must be entwined; that there is no more joy than in her joy, no sorrow but when she grieves; that in her sigh of love, in her smile of fondness, hereafter is all bliss; to feel our flaunty ambition fade away like a shrivelled gourd before her vision; to feel fame a juggle and posterity a lie; and to be prepared at once, for this great object, to forfeit and fling away all former hopes, ties, schemes, views; to violate in her favour every duty of society; this is a lover, and this is love.

Magnificent, sublime, divine sentiment! An immortal flame burns in the breast of that man who adores and is adored. He is an ethereal being. The accidents of earth touch him not. Revolutions of empire, changes of creed, mutations of opinion, are to him but the clouds and meteors of a stormy sky. The schemes and struggles of mankind are, in his thinking, but the anxieties of pigmies and the fantastical achievements of apes. Nothing can subdue him. He laughs alike at loss of fortune, loss of friends, loss of character. The deeds and thoughts of men are to him equally indifferent. He does not mingle in their paths of callous bustle, or hold himself responsible to the airy impostures before which they bow down. He is a mariner, who, in the sea of life, keeps his gaze fixedly on a single star; and, if that do not shine, he lets go the rudder, and glories when his barque descends into the bottomless gulf.

BENJAMIN DISRAELI
Henrietta Temple, 1837

ALFRED STEVENS
Mary Ann, Wife of Leonard Collman, c 1854

Love lives beyond
The tomb, the earth, which fades like dew!
I love the fond,
The faithful, and the true.

Love lives in sleep,
The happiness of healthy dreams:
Eve's dews may weep,
But love delightful seems.

'Tis seen in flowers,
And in the morning's pearly dew;
In earth's green hours,
And in the heaven's eternal blue.

'Tis heard in Spring
When light and sunbeams, warm and kind,
On angel's wing
Bring love and music to the mind . . .

Love lives beyond
The tomb, the earth, the flowers, and dew;
I love the fond,
The faithful, young and true.

JOHN CLARE
Life and Remains, 1873

HENRY ALEXANDER BOWLER
The Doubt: 'Can these Dry Bones live?' 1855

And now what monarch would not gardener be,
My fair Amanda's stately gait to see?
How her feet tempt! how soft and light she treads,
Fearing to wake the flowers from their beds!
Yet from their sweet green pillows everywhere,
They start and gaze about to see my Fair.
Look at yon flower yonder, how it grows
Sensibly! how it opes its leaves and blows,
Puts its best Easter clothes on, neat and gay:
Amanda's presence makes it holiday!
Look how on tiptoe that fair lily stands
To look on thee, and court thy whiter hands
To gather it! I saw in yonder crowd –
That tulip bed of which Dame Flora's proud –
A short dwarf flower did enlarge its stalk,
And shoot an inch to see Amanda walk . . .
The knot-grass and the daisies catch thy toes,
To kiss my fair one's feet before she goes;
All court and wish me lay Amanda down,
And give my dear a new green-flowered gown.
    Come, let me kiss thee falling, kiss at rise,
    Thou in the garden, I in Paradise.

NICHOLAS HOOKES
'Amanda', 1653

ALBERT MOORE
A Garden, 1869

There is a willow grows aslant a brook,
That shows his hoar leaves in the glassy stream:
There with fantastic garlands did she come,
Of crow-flowers, nettles, daisies and long purples,
That liberal shepherds give a grosser name,
But our cold maids do dead men's fingers call them;
There, on the pendent boughs her coronet weeds
Clambering to hang, an envious sliver broke;
When down her weedy trophies and herself
Fell in the weeping brook. Her clothes spread wide,
And, mermaid-like, awhile they bore her up:
Which time she chanted snatches of old tunes,
As one incapable of her own distress,
Or like a creature native and indued
Unto that element: but long it could not be
Till that her garments, heavy with their drink,
Pulled the poor wretch from her melodious lay
To muddy death.

WILLIAM SHAKESPEARE
Hamlet, Act IV, Scene VII

SIR JOHN EVERETT MILLAIS
Ophelia, 1851–2

Remember me when I am gone away,
Gone far away into the silent land;
When you can no more hold me by the hand,
Nor I half turn to go, yet turning stay,
Remember me when no more, day by day,
You tell me of our future that you plann'd:
Only remember me: you understand
It will be too late to counsel then or pray . . .

CHRISTINA ROSSETTI
Goblin Market and Other Poems, 1862

PHILIP HERMOGENES CALDERON
Broken Vows, 1856

Through youth and age, in love excelling,
  We'll hand in hand together tread;
Sweet-smiling peace shall crown our dwelling,
  And babes, sweet-smiling babes, our bed.

How should I love the pretty creatures,
  While round my knees they fondly clung,
To see them look their mother's features,
  To hear them lisp their mother's tongue!

And, when with envy Time transported
  Shall think to rob us of our joys,
You'll in your girls again be courted,
  And I'll go wooing in my boys.

ANONYMOUS
Miscellaneous Poems by Several Hands, 1726

JOHAN ZOFFANY
The Bradshaw Family, 1769

ACKNOWLEDGEMENTS

The publishers gratefully acknowledge permission to reproduce the following
copyright material:

William Plomer (Ed),
Kilvert's Diaries
reprinted by permission of Mrs Sheila Hooper and Jonathan Cape Limited.

Llewelyn Powys,
Love and Death
reprinted by permission of The Society of Authors
as literary representatives of the Estate of Llewelyn Powys.